JAN. 8, 2005

To My Beloved
Sister Patti,
I will love,
and cherish you

Love, Willy

To My Sister

Down through the years, we've shared so many special blessings, so many days and deeply personal feelings, so many joys and precious thoughts. Our closeness tells its own beautiful story, and it is one that will warm our hearts forever.

— Laurel Atherton

Blue Mountain Arts®
Bestselling Titles

By Susan Polis Schutz:
To My Daughter, with Love, on the Important Things in Life
To My Son, with Love
I Love You

Is It Time to Make a Change?
by Deanna Beisser

To the Love of My Life
by Donna Fargo

100 Things to Always Remember... and One Thing to Never Forget
For You, Just Because You're Very Special to Me
To the One Person I Consider to Be My Soul Mate
by Douglas Pagels

A Lifetime of Love ...Poems on the Passages of Life
by Leonard Nimoy

Anthologies:
Always Believe in Yourself and Your Dreams
For You, My Daughter
I Love You, Mom
I'm Glad You Are My Sister
May You Always Have an Angel by Your Side
Marriage Is a Promise of Love
Take Each Day One Step at a Time
Teaching and Learning Are Lifelong Journeys
There Is Greatness Within You, My Son
Think Positive Thoughts Every Day
To My Child
With God by Your Side ...You Never Have to Be Alone

Between Two

Sisters

Heartfelt notes of love and appreciation

Edited by Douglas Pagels

Blue Mountain Press ™
Boulder, Colorado

Library of Congress Control Number: 2003111801
ISBN: 0-88396-685-9

Certain trademarks are used under license.

Manufactured in China.
First Printing: 2004

 This book is printed on recycled paper.

This book is printed on fine quality, laid embossed, 80 lb. paper. This paper has been specially produced to be acid free (neutral pH) and contains no groundwood or unbleached pulp. It conforms with all the requirements of the American National Standards Institute, Inc., so as to ensure that this book will last and be enjoyed by future generations.

Blue Mountain Arts, Inc.

P.O. Box 4549, Boulder, Colorado 80306

Contents

The Story of
Two Very
Different Sisters

One is here, one is there. One is a little taller than the other. Two different styles of hair, two different outlooks on life, two very different views from their windows. Both have different tomorrows ahead.

Each is unique in so many ways. Each has her own story, with all the busy things going on in the present. Each has different work to do and different demands on the day. Each has a separate destination and a distinctly different path to get there. But...

For all the things that might be
different and unique about them...
these two sisters will always share so
much. They will always be the best of
family <u>and</u> friends, entwined together,
through all the days of their lives.
Their love will always be very special:
gentle and joyful when it can be,
strong and giving when it needs to
be, reminding them, no matter how
different their stories turn out...

They share the incredibly precious gift of being "sisters." And when you think of some of the best things this world has to offer, a blessing like that is really... what it's all about.

— Laurel Atherton

What Is a Sister?

A sister is someone more special than words. She's love mixed with friendship; the best things in life. She's so much inner beauty blended together with an outward appearance that brings a smile to the happiness in your heart...

A sister is one of the most precious people in the story of your life. And you'll always be together, whether you're near or apart.

Together, you have shared some of the most special moments two people have ever shared. A sister is a perspective on the past, and she's a million favorite memories that will always last...

A sister is a reminder of the blessings
that come from closeness. Sharing
secrets. Disclosing dreams. Learning
about life together.

A sister is a confidante and a counselor.
She's a dear and wonderful friend, and
— in certain ways — something like
a twin. She's a hand within your hand;
she's so often the only one who
really understands...

A sister is honesty and trust enfolded with love. She's sometimes the only person who sees the horizon from your point of view, and she helps you to see things more clearly. She is a helper and a guide, and she is a feeling, deep inside, that makes you wonder what you would ever do without her.

What is a sister? She's someone more special than words; someone beautiful and unique. And in so many ways, there is no one who is loved so dearly.

— Mia Evans

Thanks, Sister, for All the Smiles You've Given Me

I want you to know how amazing you are.
I want you to know how much you're
treasured and celebrated and quietly thanked.

I want you to feel really good...
     about who you are.
About all the great things you do!
I want you to appreciate your uniqueness.
Acknowledge your talents and abilities.
Realize what a beautiful soul you have.
Understand the wonder within.

You make so much sun shine through, and
you inspire so much joy in the lives of
everyone who is lucky enough to know you...

You are a very special person, giving so many people a reason to smile. You deserve to receive the best in return, and one of my heart's favorite hopes is that the happiness you give away will come back to warm you each and every day of your life.

— Sydney Nealson

What Do Sisters Share?

Invaluable feelings. Warm memories.
Acceptance. Caring. So much gratitude.

An appreciation of differences.
A celebration of similarities.
Milestones and steppingstones.
The blessing of being from a place
called "home." Life stories that are
so much alike...

The sweetness of having a best friend for life. Precious knowledge. "Inside" jokes. The perfect freedom of opening up to someone who's always there for you. A companionship that's clear to everyone. The fun of looking at photos from days gone by. Arms around one another's shoulders. Being able to lean on each other to this very day. Talking, listening, leaning, and supporting, every step of the way...

Making sure that happiness comes and sadness goes. Emotions that run deep and remain true. Loyalty. Praise. Appreciation. Hope. Giving those invaluable kinds of things. And getting countless smiles in return...

Simply enjoying all that safe, gracious familiarity. The serenity. The beauty. The joy of it all.

A trust that is so strong. A bridge that is so steady. A never-out-of-touch kind of love.

If they're really, really lucky, sisters get to share all the wonderful things

...that you and I
have so much
of.

— Marin McKay

Sister, This Is for You

I don't know exactly what it is... but there is something *very special* about you.

It might be all the things I see on the surface; things that everyone notices and admires about you. Qualities and capabilities. Your wonderful smile, obviously connected to a warm and loving heart. It might be all the things that set you apart from everyone else.

Maybe it's the big things: The way you never hesitate to go a million miles out of your way to do what's right. The way your todays help set the stage for so many beautiful tomorrows. Or maybe it's the little things: Words shared heart to heart. An unspoken understanding. Sharing seasons. Making some very wonderful memories. The joys of two people just being on the same page in one another's history...

If I could ever figure out all the magic that makes you so special, I'd probably find out that it's a combination of all these things — blended together with the best this world has to offer: Family, friendship and love, dreams come true, strong feelings, gentle talks, listening, laughing, and simply knowing someone whose light shines brighter than any star.

Sister, you really are amazing.

And I feel very lucky to have been given
the gift of knowing
how special
you are.

— Terry Bairnson

Sometimes you feel like a gift that was given to my days to make sure that they would always have some happiness in them. More than once, I have felt that what I lack in life, I make up for by having a sister like you.

I have dreams in my life that may never come true, travels I may never take, goals I may not be able to reach, and hopes that might always be just beyond my horizons. But I want you to know that whether my wishes come true or whether they disappear altogether, I will always feel like one of *the* luckiest people in the world.

Because we're going to be sisters — forever.

— Kelly Lise

As long as I live, I will consider the closeness we share to be one of the most precious gifts I could ever receive.

— L. N. Mallory

When it comes to telling you
how thankful I am for all that
you do, the words don't come
easily. I'm not sure that there
are words that reach as high as
my love, that go as deep as my
appreciation, or that can describe
something so precious.

But I can tell you this...

What you and I share within
the caring and the love and the
treasure of our family... means
the world to me.

— Denise Wills

We have a closeness that doesn't need to be measured in miles. Ours is the warm and sharing kind that has always been measured in memories made, reassurance given, and the nicest kind of smiles anyone could ask for. You are a big part of my life, and you always will be.

And I don't know what I did to deserve such a great sister, but whatever it was... I hope you know that I treasure you *so much*, and I'm eternally grateful that we are "family."

— Lorrie Westfall

Having a Sister like You
Is the Sweetest Blessing
of My Life...

There are many blessings to count in this world; good things and special people who keep smiles in the heart.

I have friends who are wonderful to me. I have people I can talk to and trust. And relations whose common bonds will always be interwoven with love and togetherness...

But as radiant and as wondrous as even
the very best people can be, no one
will ever hold a candle to you.

Sister, you are the answer to a prayer I
never even got a chance to say. I was
given this gift from the beginning of
my days — and the older I get, the
more clear the reason becomes to me.

I think that God just knew that there
would be so many times when I'd need
the blessing of a beautiful sister like you.

And I lovingly keep discovering
how precious that blessing is.

— Marta Best

I'm not going to be one of those
people whose life is filled with regrets.
Who never got around to saying what
was in her heart — and sharing what
was on her mind.

I'm not going to be one of those
people who waited for the perfect
moment — only to find that it never
managed to come around. I'm not
going to be one of those people
who looks back, years from now, and
remembers so much that was unsaid...
when there was so much
that was so important
to say...

I'm very thankful for a chance to let you know how much this bond means to me. I love the way our lives blend together so beautifully. You're the only one I'll talk to about certain things. You're the only one who gets to know how smart I've felt or how dumb I've been.

You're the only person in the universe who can dry my tears over the phone. Sometimes I see aspects of you in me (those are my best features!) and I even solve problems by wondering what you would do, and then doing the same.

Never forget what a treasure you are. That special person in the mirror may not always get to hear all the compliments you so sweetly deserve, but
    you are so worthy of such
        an abundance
           ...of thanks and joy and love.

— Robin Kelsey

I promise that I'll thank every wishing star that ever shined for bringing your closeness and understanding to me.

I promise that nothing will ever change the amount of appreciation I have for you. I promise that if I ever have news to share, you'll always be first on the call list. I promise — if I ever release a genie from a magic lamp — I'll share my three wishes with you. In the event that never happens, I promise that you're welcome to split any pizza I might have in my possession. (And the same goes for chocolate.)

I promise I will be there to see you through anything that tries to get you down. I promise that I'll be around through it all; I'll support you in your efforts; I'll believe in you at all times; we'll do whatever it takes and together we'll chase away the clouds and keep the sun shining in our lives.

— Jean Roberts

In your happiest and most exciting moments,
    my heart will celebrate and smile beside you.
In your lowest lows, my love will be there to
    keep you warm, to give you strength, and
    to remind you that your sunshine is sure
        to come again.
In your moments of accomplishment, I will
    be filled so full of pride that I may have
    a hard time keeping the feeling inside
        of me.

In your moments of disappointment, I will
    be a shoulder to cry on, a hand to hold,
    and a love that will gently enfold you
    until everything's okay.
In your gray days, I will help you search,
    one by one, for the colors of the rainbow.

— Alicia Newell

As sisters, we share something that I dearly love. It's a place of long-time understanding. Of going beyond. Of knowing all, and caring so much because of it. It's a place where we are free to be human beings — who don't always get it right, but who always find acceptance, hope, and encouragement.

As sisters, our relationship exists in a place where we wish together on one another's stars, no matter where we are.

— Gillian Reese

One of the most special
places in my heart will always be
  saved for you.
You...
 the one person I can always talk to;
 the one person who understands.
You...
 for making me laugh in the rain;
 for helping me shoulder my troubles.
You...
 for loving me in spite of myself,
 and always putting me
  back on my feet again.
You...
 for giving me someone to believe in;
 someone who lets me know that
 there really is goodness
  and kindness
   and laughter and love
    in the world.
You...
 for being one of the best
 parts of my life, and proving it
  over and over again.

      — Robin Hardt

A sister is a blessing and a miracle.
A sister is a guiding light. A sister is
a reminder that everything is all right.
Sisters always seem to understand.
They do more than hear; they listen.
They smooth out the rough edges
and offer a hand.

Sisters share: their shortcomings. Their
highest hopes. Their serious thoughts.
Their silliest jokes. Sisters are where
honesty comes from and where wishes
go. Being with a sister is what it really
means to feel at home.

— Lucy Warner

Think of This
Whenever You
Think of Me

I am with you always, and if you should
ever wonder if you are in my thoughts,
    please remember:

You are not only in my thoughts, but
you are always found... in my hopes,
keeping my heart happy, inspiring my
smile, and gracing my favorite wishes
    and memories...

Wherever you journey,
and however your day may be,
part of me is there with you
    as you... are here
        with me.

— Jenn Davids

To a Sister So Dearly Loved by Me

Down through the years, we've shared so many special blessings, so many days and deeply personal feelings, so many joys and precious thoughts. Our closeness tells its own beautiful story, and it is one that will warm our hearts forever...

Our two lives have blended together in a wonderful way. The pages of our story have unfolded with each other's hopes and dreams in mind, and ever since the early days of our endearment, we have quietly understood that what we have been given... is an exquisite and lasting gift.

So many passages have been full of laughter to share and special times to remember. Our story takes me back to memories that can still bring me a thousand smiles and make my heart more thankful for you than you can imagine...

During times when it might have appeared that life was coming apart at the seams, we always did our best to make sure we were there for each other, sharing strength, drying any tears that needed to fall, always helping one another through it all.

In life's quiet times, when I'm alone with my thoughts, I think of all the appreciation I have for you. It brings me an unspeakable joy to...

think of how strong and sure
our family ties are and to know
that, in the course of time, we
will keep adding to our story
and filling it with more caring
and togetherness than most
people could ever imagine.

In the promise of everything life
brings to me... nothing is more
beautiful than having you as
my sister.

— Laurel Atherton

I love the fact that I can just be myself with you. That's something that seems to be so difficult with other people I know, and yet it is so natural and easy with you.

It's hard to explain how much that means to me, but trust me: it is absolutely invaluable. It means that you and I have a special affinity that is bridged with complete honesty and trust. When I'm with you, I don't have to put all my feelings through a filtering process before I share them. You let me speak my mind and say what's in my heart without my having to worry about what you'll think of me if I say the wrong thing...

And even better than that... is the fact that this understanding is a two-way street. You can be just as spontaneous and as open with me, and you know that I would never do anything to alter that special flow of joy and warmth and trust that goes between us.

— Jenn Davids

There Is So Much
that Is So Precious
Between the Two of Us...

The love that exists between us is like
a very rare and beautiful flower. It's
there, no matter what. It weathers the
storms, it bends in the breeze, it
blossoms in every season of the year,
and it stays near me everywhere I go.

The sharing that exists between us is
like a foundation in my life. Upon
it, I have built so many feelings and
enjoyed so many experiences with you.
I have counted on your sharing for
strength — and I have never been
disappointed. I have relied on it for
security, and I have found more
reassurance than my words can say...

And so often, I find myself depending on the bond between us, because it has been the basis for a special trust that I share with you alone.

The happiness that exists between us is like a gift, one that seems to have been given to me to make sure that my heart would always be full and my memories would always be beautiful. I have discovered that the love that you and I share is — and always will be — a treasure.

Just between you and me, Sister... I love you a lot, and I don't know what I'd ever do without you.

— Laurel Atherton

If I could weave a tapestry, tracing the
beautiful connection between you and me,
I would be able to create a masterpiece.
I would find all my favorite colors, vibrant
ones of our childhood and the more mellow
hues of our todays, threaded together with
all the feelings you have given me. Every
crease and fold my life has known would
lead me back to you; to your spirit and
your smile, and your never-ending love.
And I would count on you, like I've always
done, to tie all the loose ends together.

I wish I could weave that beautiful tapestry.
I know it would symbolize so much. But
I hope you realize, Sister, even if all I can
weave together are these words, one of
the inspirational things that always sees me
through... is my being so thankful for you.

— Kristin Bragdon

Sister-to-Sister,
Heart-to-Heart

You represent so many good things in my life! I feel such a strong connection with you, and it's such a thankful feeling to have you here, forever and always.

Sometimes I wish I could find the perfect way to tell you how much you mean to me. There are times when I find all the right words in my heart, but it's usually when you're not around to hear them.

You know me. My life is like that. My best thoughts never seem to come out like I'd love them to, and some of my most appreciative thoughts of all are the ones I have of you...

Whenever I need you, I know I can find you in my heart. It's like opening up a door to the best part of my past and a beautiful part of my present. It's like walking along with a sunrise that brightens my life so gracefully. It's like passing by the most beautiful meadow, where fields are covered in wildflowers and trees reach to the sky and shelter me. It's like wandering along secret streams that take me right to the source of so much of the sweetness in my days.

It's finding the place where I'm happiest.

It's having a sister like you.

— Jo Waggoner

Sister,
I Think of You
Every Day

You probably don't realize how important you are to me. There are times when the one thing that helps me get through the day... is thinking of you...

You bring happiness to me when the world seems to be wearing a frown. When things don't quite go as planned and my world seems upside down, my thoughts of you help to set things right again.

You are so important to me. You make me think, you make me laugh, you make me feel alive. You put things in perspective for me. You provide support and encouragement, you lessen my worries, and you increase my joys. If my life were a puzzle, you would be the one piece that was a perfect fit.

Every day... I think of you.
And I've got a million smiles
to prove it.

— Marin McKay

What Sisters Are
All About

My feelings for you wander back
through sunny days when it felt like
we had the whole world to ourselves. We
shared so much, and we cared more than
our hearts could begin to realize. At the
time, there was so much joy I took for
granted and so many things I didn't even
stop to think of. But I began to learn how
important you were to my happiness, and
that sisters are all about... love.

As we grew, and time passed by, we had
to begin to choose the paths our lives
would take. It wasn't easy to know which
way to go and what things to do, but I
was reassured because of the treasure I
held in my heart...

By being my sister, you gave me the quiet comfort of knowing I could always turn to you. That's what sisters are all about... sweetness and support to see you through.

All through our years, you have been a source of so many smiles and so much inspiration for me. There has never been a time when the miles that came between us have not been bridged by the closeness of our hearts. I want to thank you for giving me the special kind of feelings that only sisters like you and I could comprehend. That's what sisters are all about... being the very best of friends.

— Marin McKay

To you, my sister:

For keeping my spirits up.
For never letting me down.
For being here for me.
For knowing I'm there for you.

For bringing so many smiles my way.
For being sensitive to my needs.
For knowing just what to say.
For listening better than anyone else.

For bringing me laughter.
For bringing me light.
For understanding so much about me.
For trusting me with so much about you.

For being the best.
For being so beautiful.

I don't know what I'd do
...without you.

— Joli Broeks

Remember that You Can Always Count on Me

When life isn't easy and you wonder if anyone understands what you're going through, I want you... to reach out to me. Even if we find ourselves miles apart, don't ever forget that my heart is filled with so many hopes for your happiness.

I want you to feel like you can tell me everything that's on your mind. I want to be able to help you find a million more smiles and make your days more joyful and filled with all the serenity you so dearly deserve...

When you wonder if there is anyone who cares completely and unconditionally, look my way. Let down your guard, and know that it's okay to bare your soul with someone who knows you as well as I do. When you need to talk things out, realize that you'll find a very loving listener... in me.

It doesn't matter what it's for; if it's important to you, then it's important to me. What matters most is that you gently remember: Sometimes two heads (and two hearts) are better than one, and you can always count on me to be there for you.

— Sandy Jamison

"Things You Never Knew"

You're more than just a sister to me.
You're like summer in my heart.
Warming everything.
Encouraging my world to blossom
and grow...

You let me know that smiles are to
be expected, and gifts like honesty,
closeness, laughter, and kind,
open-minded communication
will always breeze into my life
through the open doors that you
lovingly hold the key to.

My life would be so much less if
you weren't in it. I'm sorry if I
haven't expressed that thought as
much as I should have. There are
probably too many special things
that I've let go unsaid.

But of all the things you never
knew, I want to say now
that every passing year fills
my world — and my heart —

with more and more love
...for you.

— Allison Alexander

Between Two Sisters

What matters most
in the feelings of
closeness and love
between two sisters
is not that they need
to always be together...

What matters
is knowing that they
will never, ever
really be
apart.

— Anna Tafoya

Sister, maybe someday I'll be able to find all the right words to tell you how much you mean to me. In the meantime, I just hope you know, deep within your heart, that having you as my sister is a gift I thank my lucky stars for.

You're such a precious part of my life. Our family ties and our deep, lasting friendship comprise a special love that sees me through everything. If I hadn't been blessed with such a beautiful sister, I would have spent a lifetime... wishing for someone just like you.

— Jude Hopkins

"Sister Wishes"

I would give anything for these wishes
to keep coming true for us
        all our lives...

That we may always be more than close.
That nothing will ever come between
    the bond of love we're blessed with.
That we will celebrate our similarities,
    honor the things that make each of
    us unique, and quietly realize that
    every part of the circle of our lives
        is a special, precious gift.

That I will always be here for you,
    as you will be for me.
That we will listen with love...

That we will share everything that
    wants to — and needs to — be shared.
That we will care unconditionally.

That we will trust so much, and we will
    talk things out.
That we will nurture each other's
    spirits and warm each other's souls.
That even when no one else knows
    what's going on inside...
    you and I will gently understand...

...And that wherever you go, you will be
in my heart, and my hand
will be in your hand.

— Katie Russell